Glistening Tranquility

Lights twinkle in the night,
Joyful laughter fills the air,
Wrapped in warmth, hearts ignite,
Moments cherished, beyond compare.

Snowflakes dance as music plays,
Children's voices, pure delight,
The magic weaves through joyful days,
In the glow of the soft moonlight.

Midnight Frost

Stars are bright, a silver glow,
Whispers soft on frosty breeze,
Nature sparkles, oh so slow,
Winter's charm brings hearts to ease.

Carols echo through the trees,
Peaceful nights in purest grace,
Each note carried by the freeze,
In this still and tranquil place.

Stillness Beneath Evergreens

Beneath tall pines, the world is bright,
Softly nestled in the snow,
Sprigs of holly, pure delight,
In this quiet we will grow.

Candles flicker, shadows play,
Warmth surrounds with every glance,
The spirit of this festive day,
Invites us all to join the dance.

A Blanket of Peace

Fields of white, a shimmering sheet,
Peace descends, a gentle sigh,
Hands entwined, hearts skip a beat,
Underneath the starlit sky.

Fireside tales, old and new,
Sharing moments, warm and bright,
Wishes whispered, hopes that grew,
A blanket wraps us through the night.

Slumbering Woods

In the heart of the woods, life breathes slow,
Whispers of joy in the soft, gentle flow.
Colorful leaves dance, twirling around,
Nature's own music, a magical sound.

Beneath the tall pines, children all play,
Laughter and cheer brighten up the day.
Sunlight sifts through, a golden delight,
In the slumbering woods, all feels just right.

Twilight's Shimmer

As twilight descends, the stars start to gleam,
Softly they twinkle, like dreams in a dream.
Fireflies flicker in sync with the light,
A festival of wonders, pure and bright.

Families gather around fires aglow,
Sharing sweet stories, and laughter in tow.
Shadows dance lightly, embraced by a sigh,
In twilight's shimmer, the moments fly high.

Snowflakes and Serenity

The world wrapped in white, a quilt oh so fine,
Snowflakes are falling, a soft, gentle line.
Children all bundled, they frolic with glee,
Building their snowmen, as happy as can be.

Hot cocoa waiting, steam rising in curls,
Such warmth in the air as the magic unfurls.
Winter's embrace, with serenity wrapped,
In snowflakes and joy, we happily tapped.

Hibernal Reflections

In the chill of the night, the stars brightly shine,
Gathered together, all souls intertwine.
Stories ignite as the embers grow low,
Within hibernal dreams, we're never alone.

The warmth of the hearth, a comforting glow,
Fireside laughter, as gentle winds blow.
Each moment is cherished, shared hearts intertwine,
In hibernal reflections, our spirits align.

Serenity Beneath the Stars

In a night of laughter and light,
The stars shimmer, casting delight.
Colorful lanterns dance in the air,
Joyful whispers, a moment to share.

Music plays softly, hearts intertwine,
With every note, spirits brightly shine.
Families gather, stories unfold,
A tapestry woven with joy untold.

Sweets and treats fill up the table,
Each little bite, a cherished fable.
Laughter erupts like fireworks bright,
Together we bask in the warm moonlight.

As the evening drifts gently away,
Promises linger in the soft sway.
Serenity here beneath the stars,
A festive night, a world of ours.

Echoes of a Frozen World

In the stillness, snowflakes fall,
Dressing the world in a glittering shawl.
Children's laughter fills the air,
As winter's magic we all share.

Fires crackle with warmth so bright,
Creating shadows that dance in the night.
Hot cocoa steams in every hand,
Uniting hearts across the land.

The shimmering lights twinkle and glow,
Each sparkling moment begins to flow.
Songs of the season rise in cheer,
Echoes of joy that we hold dear.

Under the moon, the world feels small,
In this frozen realm, we are all.
The festive spirit wraps us tight,
Echoes of a world filled with light.

Stillness in the Air

In the glow of twilight's grace,
Laughter dances, hearts embraced.
Colors whirl, like stars in flight,
Joyful whispers spark the night.

Beneath the lantern's gentle gleam,
Hope ignites, a vibrant dream.
Every face with smiles aglow,
In this warmth, our spirits flow.

.

Whispering Pines

Underneath the tall, green trees,
Voices hum upon the breeze.
Children play with glee and cheer,
As nature's song unfolds so clear.

Branches sway with secrets old,
Stories shared, like threads of gold.
In this realm of joy divine,
With every heartbeat, we align.

Hushed Footprints

Through the snow, we leave our trace,
A path of warmth, a dance of grace.
Laughter echoes, soft and bright,
As we cherish this pure night.

Twinkling lights on every street,
Melodies in the rhythmic beat.
Together, we embrace the cheer,
In the hush, our hearts are near.

Crystal Calm

With shimmered frost on windowpanes,
Every moment joy retains.
Chimes of laughter fill the air,
Glowing spirits everywhere.

Candles flicker, shadows play,
In this magic, we'll stay.
Each smile shared, a precious gem,
In the stillness, love's our hem.

Silent Whispers of Frost

Whispers of frost in the chilly air,
Laughter and joy spread without a care.
Twinkling lights dance on branches bare,
Together we gather, a moment to share.

Candles aglow in the crisp night sky,
Children delight, time seems to fly.
Carols ring out, hearts lifting high,
Love binds us close, as stars twinkle by.

A Blanket of Stillness

A blanket of stillness, nature's soft breath,
Covering silence, a peaceful caress.
Snowflakes are falling, in white they are dressed,
Under the moonlight, all troubles suppressed.

Firesides crackle, warm stories unfold,
In the heart of winter, we cherish the cold.
Friends by the hearth, with laughter retold,
Creating sweet memories, more precious than gold.

Dreams Draped in Snow

Dreams draped in snow, a sight to behold,
Whispers of magic in the air unfold.
Footsteps in powder, a canvas of gold,
Each path that we wander, a story retold.

Ice skates are gliding on shimmering lakes,
Joy fills the air, with every move takes.
Hot cocoa shared, as laughter awakes,
In this festive moment, the heart finally breaks.

Beneath the Frosted Sky

Beneath the frosted sky, the world stands still,
Frosted trees glimmer with winter's goodwill.
Voices of children echo over the hill,
In the spirit of joy, our hearts are fulfilled.

Gaily we sing, 'neath the twinkling lights,
Uniting our souls on these magical nights.
Together we dance, as the world ignites,
In love and in laughter, our spirits take flight.

Ethereal Silence

A shimmer hush covers the ground,
With whispered dreams that dance around.
The soft glow of lanterns fills the air,
As laughter echoes, it lingers there.

Joyous hearts in a twinkling sight,
With every glance, the world feels right.
Beneath the stars, the secrets twine,
In this moment, all souls align.

Calmness in the Cold

The winter chill brings warmth to cheer,
In frosted breath, we hold each dear.
With mugs of joy and ginger spice,
The cold feels warm, the world feels nice.

Crisp laughter dances in the night,
As snowflakes twirl in gentle flight.
Together we gather, hearts aglow,
In this calmness, we let love flow.

Starlit Whispers

Under skies draped in velvet light,
We share our dreams, hearts taking flight.
The celestial dance, a grand parade,
In starlit whispers, memories made.

Together we twirl on this cosmic floor,
Each laugh and hug, an open door.
With wishes cast on a gentle breeze,
The universe sighs in perfect ease.

A Pause in Time

In the midst of joy, we take a breath,
As laughter rings, we forget the rest.
This moment suspended, a soft embrace,
In the warmth of friends, we find our place.

The world may spin outside our space,
But here, it's just a joyful grace.
With time as our play, we dance and sway,
In this pause forever, let's gently stay.

Frozen Whispers of Time

In the chill of twilight's glow,
Snowflakes twirl, a gentle show.
Laughter echoes, hearts ignite,
Frozen whispers in the night.

Candles flicker, warmth in hand,
Joyful spirits fill the land.
Voices blend in soft embrace,
Magic weaves through every space.

Time stands still, a fleeting dream,
Life awash in silver gleam.
Moments cherished, memories share,
Frozen whispers fill the air.

Illuminated by Moonlit Snow

Beneath a blanket, pure and bright,
Moonlight dances, soft delight.
Crystals shimmer, night aglow,
Illuminated by moonlit snow.

Footprints lead on shimmering trails,
Echoes of laughter fill the gales.
Children's joy, boundless and free,
In this wonder, unity.

Hearts entwined in festive cheer,
Memories linger, ever dear.
With every step, we find our way,
Through moonlit nights, in bright array.

A Dance of Broken Icicles

With a shatter, they greet the ground,
Icicles sing a lively sound.
Nature's rhythm, frost's embrace,
A dance of joy in this space.

Colors burst, as laughter soars,
In the chill, the spirit roars.
Each fragment shines, a tale told,
Of festive nights and friendships bold.

In the warmth of firelight's glow,
Stories shared in winter's show.
Broken icicles, life shall weave,
In this festival, let's believe.

Quietude in the Shivering Woods

In the woods where shadows play,
Softly drifts the end of day.
A hush befalls, the world serene,
Quietude in hues of green.

Snowflakes cradle whispers low,
Gentle secrets shared in flow.
Nature pauses, breaths anew,
In quietude, we find the true.

The starry canvas starts to glow,
Underneath, the world in tow.
Amidst the shiver, warmth resides,
Joyful hearts where magic thrives.

Twilight's Embrace

The sun dips low, a golden wave,
Filling the skies with colors brave.
Laughter dances on the air,
As joy ignites our hearts to share.

Twinkling lights begin to glow,
Whispers of warmth in the night show.
Friends gather round with cheerful glee,
In twilight's embrace, we feel so free.

Glistening Moments

Snowflakes twirl in the crisp night air,
Each one unique, a moment rare.
Smiles abound, like stars in sight,
All hearts aglow in pure delight.

With every sip of cocoa warm,
We find a cozy, loving charm.
Laughter rings like chimes of cheer,
In glistening moments, we draw near.

Heartbeats of Winter

The world slows down, a gentle hush,
As winter paints in a silver brush.
Candles flicker, casting light,
While shadows dance through the night.

With every heartbeat, warmth we feel,
In shared stories, our hearts reveal.
Together we embrace the chill,
In winter's heart, we find our thrill.

Solace in Silence

Beneath the stars, a tranquil peace,
Where worries fade and joys increase.
In the silence, whispers flow,
Like gentle streams in moonlit glow.

Each moment held, a treasure dear,
In solace found, we shed each fear.
Together in this still embrace,
We find our hearts, our sacred space.

Cozy Corners

In the glow of twinkling light,
Laughter dances through the night.
Friends gather close, tales unfold,
Warmth surrounds where hearts are bold.

Cider simmers, spices blend,
Joy and cheer, a loving trend.
Soft blankets draped on each chair,
Embracing smiles, a love to share.

Veils of Frost

Snowflakes twirl like gentle dreams,
Nature wrapped in frosty beams.
The world glimmers in white lace,
Every corner, a magic space.

Children's laughter fills the air,
Snowmen stand with frosty flair.
Hot cocoa warms both hands and heart,
In this season, we won't part.

Nature's Breath

The trees whisper in hushed tones,
Swaying soft, their ancient bones.
Birds return with joyful song,
Nature's pulse where we belong.

Colors burst, a painter's glee,
Life awakens, wild and free.
Sunshine blankets every patch,
In this moment, spirits match.

Calm Before the Thaw

A stillness wraps the quiet land,
Icicles hang like crystal strands.
The air holds breath, serene and bright,
Waiting for spring's promise of light.

Fires crackle, embers glow,
Whispers of warmth in the snow.
We cherish this soft lull,
Before life's dance begins to pull.

Threads of Silence in the Air

In the glow of twinkling lights,
Laughter dances through the night.
Shadows waltz in colors bright,
Joyful whispers take their flight.

Crisp air hums with secret cheer,
Gathered friends hold moments dear.
Each glance sparkles, hearts sincere,
Together we shall persevere.

Songs of love, sweet melodies,
Fleeting minutes on the breeze.
As stardust falls from the trees,
Life's a canvas that we seize.

With every cheer and festive toast,
We celebrate, we laugh the most.
In our hearts, we raise a host,
To cherish moments we love most.

The Kiss of Morning Frost

Dewdrops glisten, a pristine sheet,
Nature wraps in white, so sweet.
Footsteps crunch on frosty ground,
In this silence, joy is found.

Trees adorned with icy lace,
Every branch wears winter's grace.
Sunrise kisses the cold air,
Awakening dreams everywhere.

Hot cocoa warms the chilly hands,
Laughter mingles, life expands.
A festival of cheer and light,
Morning shines, festive and bright.

As we gather, hearts entwined,
In every moment, love we find.
Together here, a bond defined,
In nature's peace, our souls aligned.

Tranquil Echoes of Forgotten Fables

Beneath the stars, old tales are spun,
Whispers of magic, stories begun.
The night air carries joy's sweet sound,
In enchanting circles, we gather 'round.

Lanterns flicker, guiding the way,
Laughter mingles as children play.
Dreams unfold in the soft twilight,
In the arms of the gentle night.

Voices rise like the moon above,
Wrapped in warmth, surrounded by love.
Every heart beats in rhythmic time,
Together, we weave the perfect rhyme.

Old fables find new life tonight,
In our hearts, they shine so bright.
Through memories shared, we take flight,
In tranquil echoes, pure delight.

Beneath the Veil of Ice

Crystal whispers, the world aglow,
Nature's canvas, beauty in snow.
Beneath the veil where silence lies,
Magic dances beneath the skies.

Children laughing, snowballs fly,
A season of joy, oh me, oh my!
Scents of pine and cocoa blends,
Where every moment warmth ascends.

Fireplaces crackle, stories spun,
Gathered close, the warmth begun.
Shadows flicker, our spirits rise,
Together here, a sweet surprise.

Beneath the ice, a promise grows,
In every heart, a love that glows.
We celebrate the ties that bind,
In winter's arms, our dreams unwind.

Winter's Gentle Embrace

Snowflakes dance upon the air,
Softly whispering love everywhere.
Candles flicker, warm and bright,
Gather 'round, it's pure delight.

Friends and laughter fill the room,
Joyful hearts begin to bloom.
Sipping cocoa, feeling free,
Winter's magic, just you and me.

The hearth glows with a sacred flame,
Each moment cherished, none the same.
As carols ring and spirits soar,
We celebrate what's worth living for.

Through frosty nights, our souls ignite,
In winter's grasp, all feels so right.
With every heartbeat, every cheer,
Festive warmth, as we draw near.

A Symphony of Silence

In the quiet of the night,
Stars twinkle, oh so bright.
Moonlight bathes the earth in grace,
A tranquil smile on nature's face.

Whispers soft, a gentle breeze,
Harmonies in snowy trees.
The world slows down, takes a breath,
In this stillness, we dance with depth.

Fires crackle with stories bold,
Glimmers of warmth amidst the cold.
Wrapped in blankets, cozy tight,
We find joy in pure twilight.

Embrace the night, with hearts aglow,
A symphony of silence, soft and slow.
Together we weave a festive song,
In winter's magic, we'll belong.

Nightfall's Chill

As the sun dips low and fades,
Nightfall's chill in soft cascades.
Blankets shimmering with frost,
In this quiet, warmth embossed.

Crackling fires and laughter bright,
Fill the air with pure delight.
Mugs of cider, sweetened cheer,
Every moment, we hold dear.

The stars emerge, a twinkling show,
Each a promise in the glow.
Hands held tight, beneath the sky,
In festive spirit, we fly high.

Chill may linger, yet hearts are warm,
Wrapped in love, a festive charm.
Together, through the cool of night,
We celebrate life's sweet light.

Frost-kissed Pause

Frost-kissed mornings softly gleam,
A world transformed, like a dream.
Crystal branches whisper low,
In this beauty, our spirits grow.

Children's laughter fills the air,
Snowmen standing without a care.
Sleds rush down, with shouts of glee,
Every moment, joyful and free.

Gathering close, the fire's heat,
In festive cheer, our hearts compete.
Sharing stories, old and new,
With every smile, our friendship grew.

As day turns to night, stars appear,
A frosty silence, magic near.
We pause to revel, grateful, true,
In winter's gift, me and you.

A Canvas of White

Snowflakes dance in the chilly air,
Blanketing the world with gentle care.
Children's laughter fills the streets,
Joyful moments, magical treats.

Twinkling lights adorn each home,
Warmth and cheer wherever we roam.
Hearts united, spirits bright,
In this canvas of purest white.

Carols echo through the night,
Melodies of love take flight.
Glowing fires in every heart,
From this joy, we cannot part.

As we gather, taste and share,
Celebrate the season's flair.
With every hug and every cheer,
The festive spirit draws us near.

Yuletide Stillness

In the hush of a winter night,
Stars above, oh, what a sight!
Crisp the air, so clear and bright,
Yuletide stillness, pure delight.

Families gather, candles gleam,
Whispers shared, a lovely dream.
Home is here, where love prevails,
Wrapped in warmth, where joy entails.

Cookies baking, scents unfold,
Stories shared, and memories told.
Merry faces, warmth and cheer,
Chasing all the cares from here.

A time of peace, a joyful pause,
In every heart, love gives applause.
Together now, let laughter ring,
In this season, our hearts take wing.

Crystalline Reflections

Icicles glimmer in the sun,
Nature's art, a gift for everyone.
Crystal shards reflect the light,
Joyful wonders, sparkling bright.

Every window dressed in cheer,
Festive colors drawing near.
Gifts wrapped in bows, love declared,
Peaceful moments that we're shared.

The laughter of friends fills the air,
In every smile, a depth of care.
Echoing through the frosty scene,
Crystalline sights, a vision serene.

As we toast to the night ahead,
In sweet embrace, our worries shed.
With every glance, a joyful dance,
In this festive, fleeting chance.

Ethereal Breezes

Ethereal breezes whisper low,
Carrying tales of long ago.
Snowflakes twirl, a ballet grand,
Woven dreams as we all stand.

Festive spirits rise so high,
In the twinkle of a starlit sky.
Harmonies of hope and cheer,
Bring us closer, year by year.

Wreaths adorned with ribbons bright,
Guide us in this wondrous night.
Together we share the glow,
Of cherished moments, love to grow.

With each breath of winter's grace,
We find our home in this embrace.
In the magic of the night, we find,
Ethereal breezes, hearts combined.

Essence of a Quiet Night

Stars twinkle bright in the sky,
Soft whispers of night, oh so nigh.
The moon casts a silver glow,
Peace wraps the world in a flow.

Laughter spills from distant halls,
Warmth of hearts as joy enthralls.
Cookies baked, aromas divine,
Sweet moments shared with good wine.

Crickets chirp a gentle tune,
Beneath the watchful eyes of the moon.
Fires crackle with stories told,
In this magic, we feel bold.

As night deepens, dreams take flight,
In the essence of this quiet night.
With every heartbeat, love ignites,
In the soft embrace of peaceful sights.

Muffled Murmurs

Gathered close, we share our tales,
With joyful hearts and happy gales.
Muffled murmurs floating high,
Echoing laughter, a starry sky.

Candles glow with a warm embrace,
As smiles and wishes fill the space.
The clinking glasses sing of cheer,
We celebrate those we hold dear.

Outside, the world spins in its haste,
But here, no moment goes to waste.
Togetherness wraps us like a song,
In this moment, we all belong.

Underneath a blanket of stars,
Every heartbeat feels like ours.
In the night where magic swirls,
Muffled murmurs paint our worlds.

Glacial Serenity

Snowflakes fall like tender dreams,
Silence blankets the frost-kissed streams.
Nature whispers in crystal tones,
As winter wraps the earth in bones.

Mountains loom with majesty high,
Reflecting tranquility in the sky.
The air crisp, fresh, and free,
In glacial serenity, we feel glee.

Footprints trace a gentle path,
In the stillness, we find our bath.
Each breath a vapor in the cold,
Together, warmth makes us bold.

In this quiet, life feels pure,
Wonders of nature, they allure.
With each flake, a peaceful tear,
Glacial serenity brings us near.

Calm Amidst the Storm

Winds howl, yet we hold each other tight,
The tempest rages through the night.
Yet in this chaos, hearts align,
Finding calm where stars still shine.

Raindrops dance on windowpane,
Nature's symphony, a wild refrain.
In the eye, a hush envelopes all,
Together we rise, never fall.

Fires crackle, warmth ignites,
Tales are spun through stormy nights.
With laughter echoing in the gloom,
We create light, dispelling doom.

Hold my hand as thunder rolls,
In our cocoon, we keep our goals.
Amidst the storm, we find our way,
In love's embrace, we forever stay.

Frost-kissed Moments

Snowflakes twirl like dancers bright,
Laughter echoes through the night.
Crisp and clear, the air does sing,
Joyful hearts, we gather, bringing.

Warmth of fire, a glowing cheer,
Friends and family drawing near.
With mugs of cocoa, spirits soar,
Frost-kissed moments, who could ask for more?

Glistening paths where children play,
Bright decorations on display.
Whispers of love in the chill,
Each frozen moment, a treasured thrill.

Let the stars above ignite,
Our festive spirits, pure delight.
In every laugh, in every glance,
Frost-kissed moments, life's sweet dance.

As Night Falls in White

As night falls, the world aglow,
A blanket white, soft and slow.
Candles flicker, warm and bright,
Inviting dreams, love takes flight.

Laughter rings through frosty air,
Joy and hope are everywhere.
Fires crackle, shadows play,
Together, cherished moments stay.

In the hush of gentle night,
Stars above are shining bright.
With every twinkle, wishes flow,
As night falls, our hearts will grow.

Cheers resound, as old meets new,
Festive spirits, a vibrant hue.
Holding hands, we make a vow,
To cherish moments, here and now.

Gentle Breath of the Blizzards

Winter whispers with a sigh,
Snowflakes dance from the sky.
Each breath a cloud, a puff of white,
Gentle blizzards, pure delight.

Children's laughter fills the street,
Bundled up in cozy heat.
Sleds racing down a shimmering slope,
Joyful hearts wrapped in hope.

Fires crackle with stories spun,
Each tale woven with winter's fun.
Sharing joys and cocoa sweet,
In this haven, our lives meet.

Celebrate with every cheer,
Gather close to those we hold near.
In the joy of each moment made,
The gentle breath of the blizzards played.

In the Embrace of the Cold

Embrace the cold, the air so clear,
Festive cheer is drawing near.
With each breath, the magic glows,
In winter's hug, our spirit flows.

Carols sung, the night aglow,
Magic sparkles, hearts shall grow.
Once again, our kin will meet,
In the warmth, our joys repeat.

Lights that twinkle, bright and fine,
Every corner, love will shine.
In laughter shared, in stories told,
We find our warmth in the embrace of the cold.

From the first snow to the last,
Treasured memories, ever vast.
In the chill, our hearts unite,
Together glowing, pure delight.

Lanterns Glimmering in Dusk

Lanterns sway with gentle light,
Casting dreams into the night.
Laughter dances, hearts take flight,
In the warmth, all feels just right.

Joyful chatter fills the air,
Colors bright, a vibrant fair.
Every smile, a gem to share,
Under stars, we lose our care.

Families gather, bonds grow strong,
In this moment, we belong.
Stories shared, like a sweet song,
Together here, we can't go wrong.

As dusk fades, the lanterns glow,
Embers spark, the evening slow.
In this fest, our spirits flow,
In the warmth, our love we sow.

Embracing the Chilling Silence

Snowflakes twirl in frosty air,
A silent night, free from despair.
Crisp and clear, the world so fair,
Wrapped in warmth, a tender care.

Stars above, a sparkling spree,
Nature's hush, a symphony.
Holding hands, just you and me,
In this peace, we feel so free.

Footprints trace our whispered path,
Gentle laughs, the aftermath.
Sharing stories, the night will last,
In this moment, we are cast.

With every breath, the chill retreats,
Heartbeats echo, soft and sweet.
In this silence, love completes,
Together here, our souls meet.

Petals of Ice on the Midnight Pond

Moonlight glistens on the lake,
Petals drift, soft dreams awake.
In the stillness, echoes quake,
Whispers hush, as hearts partake.

Winter's breath paints frost so light,
Beauty shines in the soft night.
Every glance, a lovely sight,
In this charm, our hopes ignite.

Reflections dance as shadows play,
Lost in magic, come what may.
Holding tight, we gently sway,
With every pulse, our hearts convey.

On this pond, we find our song,
Petals float, where we belong.
In the silence, we'll prolong,
Together here — we're ever strong.

Starlit Solitude

Underneath the starlit sky,
Whispers travel, soft and shy.
In the dark, we float and fly,
With the world, our dreams comply.

Time stands still, a calming balm,
Held in nature's soothing calm.
Every heartbeat, every psalm,
In the night, life feels like charm.

Moonlight weaves through branches wide,
Casting silver, love our guide.
In this moment, hearts collide,
Together here, we won't divide.

As the stars begin to fade,
Memories of magic made.
In this quiet serenade,
In our souls, the joy is laid.

Light of a Pale Moon

Under the glow of the pale, soft moon,
Laughter dances as evening lifts its tune.
Joyous hearts in a gentle embrace,
Whispers of magic fill this quiet space.

Stars twinkle like diamonds, all aglow,
Each flicker a promise, a warm-hearted show.
Friendship and warmth in the cool night air,
Moments like these, so precious and rare.

Candles flicker with flames that delight,
Lighting paths on this merry night.
Together we cherish this dreamlike scene,
An ode to the festive, brilliant and keen.

As shadows dance under trees strung with light,
We gather as one, hearts holding tight.
In the light of a pale moon, dreams take flight,
Capturing joy 'til the dawn's early light.

Frosty Boughs and Soft Souls

Frosty boughs bend low, adorned with white,
Nature's art crafted in shimmering light.
Children's laughter fills the chilly air,
Each gleeful shout, beyond compare.

A warm cup of cocoa in everyone's hand,
Fleeting moments, both simple and grand.
On this festive eve, we gather near,
Love and cheer banish all fear.

The scent of pine whispers through the trees,
Bringing memories carried on a breeze.
Chimes ring gently as the night wears on,
Voices unite in a sweet, joyful song.

Flakes swirl softly, dancing through space,
Each one unique, like a tender embrace.
In frost and in laughter, our hearts must stay,
Frosty boughs whispering all cares away.

Peace in the Falling Snow

Snowflakes drifting in the quiet night,
Covering the world in a blanket of white.
Hear the soft whispers of nature's delight,
Wrapped in the magic, everything feels right.

Families gather, each heart intertwined,
Stories and silence, together they find.
The firelight dances, casting warm glow,
In the comfort of home, love starts to grow.

Glistening crystals fall from the sky,
Painting the earth as the nights drift by.
In this serene calm, we find our way,
Peace in the falling snow, here we stay.

Hope in each flake, new dreams to pursue,
Promises whispered beneath skies so blue.
In the still of the night, with spirits aglow,
We celebrate life wrapped in white, soft snow.

Eloquent Echoes of Ice

Beneath the vast sky, the echoes of ice,
Whisper sweet tales, each moment a slice.
As lanterns shine bright, our shadows entwine,
In laughter and joy, we toast with good wine.

The crisp air surrounds, filled with magic and cheer,
Capturing moments as loved ones draw near.
Songs weave through the trees, where memories thrive,
Eloquent echoes keep our spirits alive.

Frost encrusted tales of laughter and love,
Remind us the blessings we're dreaming of.
As candles flicker, hearts glow with delight,
Each smile and each hug feel just perfectly right.

In these enchanted nights, our spirits can soar,
Wrapped in this wonder, we open new doors.
Eloquent echoes, we'll cherish and share,
In the warmth of the moment, everything's fair.

A Whisper of Chill

Snowflakes dance lightly in the air,
Children's laughter echoes everywhere.
Warm lights twinkle in the night,
Joyful hearts feel pure delight.

Hot cocoa served by the fire's glow,
Cozy warmth in the winter's flow.
Carols sung with voices bright,
Filling the dark with sweet invite.

Scarves wrapped tight against the breeze,
Gathered close, we share with ease.
Stories told of holidays past,
Creating memories built to last.

With every morsel of festive cheer,
Love and laughter draw us near.
In this moment, time stands still,
As whispers of chill give us thrill.

Echoes of the Frost

The frost paints art on every pane,
Nature's beauty, a soft refrain.
Footprints crunch on the frozen ground,
Echoes of joy and laughter abound.

Candles flicker in windows bright,
Filling the cold with warm delight.
Families gathered, a feast to share,
Embracing love that's everywhere.

The starry night sky shines so clear,
Wishes whispered, the season near.
Each moment cherished, hearts align,
In the echoes of frost, we intertwine.

Cheers resound as glasses clink,
To special times that make us think.
With spirits high, we all embrace,
This festive season, a warm embrace.

Frozen Dusk

As dusk descends, the world aglow,
A tapestry of white and snow.
Flickering lights on every street,
In frozen dusk, our hearts can meet.

Children play with snowball fights,
Building dreams under twinkling lights.
The air is crisp, a joyful tune,
Sung beneath the silver moon.

Fires crackle, the scent of pine,
Gathered close, our spirits shine.
With every hug and laughter shared,
In frozen dusk, love is declared.

Wrapping up in scarves so bright,
Lost in the magic of the night.
Here's to the memories we create,
In this festivity, we celebrate.

In the Heart of Stillness

In stillness, a peaceful hush,
The world slows down amidst the rush.
Snowflakes drift like whispered dreams,
In the heart of stillness, joy redeems.

Candles glow in the quiet night,
Each flame a beacon, warm and bright.
Families gather, stories shared,
In this moment, everyone cared.

The magic lingers in every glance,
In every hug, we find our chance.
To cherish love in every way,
In the heart of stillness, we sway.

So let us raise our voices high,
With laughter echoing to the sky.
In festive cheer, our spirits soar,
In the heart of stillness, we explore.

Frosted Serenity

The world adorned in silver gleam,
Joy dances like a gentle stream.
Soft whispers of a frosty night,
Embracing all in pure delight.

Laughter echoes, warm and bright,
As candles flicker, hearts take flight.
Families gather, stories share,
In the glow of love's sweet flare.

Children build their snowy dreams,
With rosy cheeks, and giggly screams.
Snowflakes waltz on winter's tune,
Underneath the gleaming moon.

In this moment, time stands still,
Wrapped in warmth, our hearts we fill.
Frosted peace, a cherished call,
Together, we have it all.

Dreams in White

Blankets of snow on rooftops lie,
Beneath the vast and starlit sky.
Whispers of dreams in frosty air,
Hope glimmers bright, beyond compare.

Children's laughter fills the night,
As snowflakes twirl in pure delight.
Hot cocoa warms our hands so tight,
Creating memories, hearts take flight.

The moonlight sparkles, laughter spills,
Through frosty lanes and snowy hills.
Mystic nights where magic flows,
In dreams of white, our spirit grows.

Festivities weave a joyful song,
In winter's embrace, we all belong.
Together we dance, in merry cheer,
Dreams in white, forever near.

Shadows in the Snow

Beneath the trees, shadows play,
In the snow, they dance away.
Footprints lead to whispered tales,
As winter's breath gently exhales.

Warm lights twinkle, spirits lift,
In the hush, we find our gift.
Sipping cider, stories flow,
As laughter mingles with the snow.

The world transforms in chilled embrace,
Each corner holds a quiet grace.
In shadows deep, a flicker bright,
Within the heart, the cheer ignites.

Nature's canvas, white and pure,
In every heart, joy knows no cure.
Shadows dance and spirits soar,
Together we cherish, forevermore.

Nature's Quiet Hand

Silence wrapped in snowy white,
Nature's hand, a pure delight.
Glistening trees in moonlit glow,
Whispers soft, as cold winds blow.

Gathered close by fireside cheer,
Voices blend, with love so near.
Stockings hung, and laughter shared,
Hearts entwined, together bared.

The world transformed, a festive scene,
As joy pours forth, like sparkling sheen.
In each flake, a wish is spun,
Uniting all, we become one.

With every glance, a moment's grace,
Nature's quiet hand we embrace.
Through winter's charm, we find our way,
In joy and peace, we celebrate.

Crisp Air of Solitary Moments

The chill of dawn breaks bright and clear,
Sparkling lights draw us near.
Laughter rings through frosty air,
In this moment, joy we share.

Each breath a cloud, a fleeting sight,
Gathering magic under soft twilight.
Footprints crunching in the fresh snow,
Together, where warm fires glow.

A lantern's glow, a friendly smile,
We walk hand in hand for a while.
Crisp air fills the heart with cheer,
In solitary moments, you feel no fear.

The quiet buzz of life around,
In winter's embrace, love is found.
Here we cherish each fleeting hour,
In nature's dance, we find our power.

Frosted Memories Through the Pines.

Beneath the trees with branches bare,
Whispers of winter fill the air.
Frosted memories intertwine,
In the stillness, hearts align.

Sunlight glistens on the frost,
Every moment, never lost.
The scent of pine, so fresh and bright,
Guiding us through the soft twilight.

Laughter echoes through the maze,
In nature's wonders, we are laid.
Snowflakes dance, a gentle tune,
Underneath the watchful moon.

Hand in hand, we stroll along,
In frosted dreams where we belong.
Through the pines, our spirits soar,
Creating memories forevermore.

Silent Snowfall

In the hush of night so deep,
Snowflakes fall as the world sleeps.
Each flake whispers a gentle theme,
Carrying dreams like a soft gleam.

Blankets of white, so pure and bright,
Transforming shadows into light.
With every drift, our worries fade,
As winter's peace begins to invade.

Children laugh in joyful play,
Building castles, dreaming away.
Silent snowfall wraps us tight,
In this magic, hearts take flight.

Underneath the starlit skies,
We find warmth in each other's eyes.
In the silence, love does call,
Embracing the joy of silent fall.

Frosty Whispers

As morning breaks with frosty breath,
Nature dons her cloak of death.
Whispers rustle through the trees,
Bringing tales on the chill wind's breeze.

Snowflakes twirl in playful dance,
Invoking memories with a glance.
Frosty patterns paint the ground,
In every corner, joy is found.

Hot cocoa warms our chilly hands,
In each sip, a world expands.
Around the fire, stories ignite,
Frosty whispers, hearts feel light.

With every cheer, we gather near,
In frosty moments, love is clear.
Together, let these memories weave,
In frosty whispers, we believe.

The Calm Before the Dawn

The night is still, the stars aglow,
Whispers of dreams begin to flow.
A chill in the air, a promise clear,
The dawn will break, our hearts will cheer.

Laughter dances in the quiet night,
Moonlight glimmers, oh what a sight.
Frosted branches, a shimmering hue,
Together we wait for skies so blue.

Each moment wraps in a gentle hold,
Stories shared, each one's a gold.
As slumber fades and daylight sings,
Hope awakens, oh what joy it brings.

With warm embraces and love so bright,
We greet the day, the world alight.
The calm before, a cherished space,
In this embrace, we find our grace.

Pathways in the Snowbound Dreams

Footprints lead through glistening white,
A journey taken under the moonlight.
Each step a song, a tale untold,
In winter's charm, our hearts unfold.

Twinkling lights on frosty trees,
Whispers of joy ride on the breeze.
Dreams wrapped tightly in snowy hugs,
A festive spirit that warmly tugs.

With friends beside, we laugh and play,
Building memories that light the way.
In every snowflake, a wish we find,
Together we weave the ties that bind.

As dawn approaches, colors ignite,
Painting the world with warmth and light.
In pathways of dreams, we dance and sway,
A festive heart beckons us to stay.

Secrets Buried Underneath Snow

Beneath the blanket, whispers lie,
Stories of laughter that never die.
Memories hidden, yet ever near,
In the snow's embrace, they reappear.

Twinkling stars in a velvet sky,
Echoes of laughter as time flies by.
Each snowdrift holds a secret so dear,
As winter wraps us, we draw near.

Fires crackle, and shadows play,
Sharing our dreams as night turns to day.
In frosty air, our voices blend,
The magic of winter, a timeless friend.

When spring arrives and melts away,
The secrets buried won't fade to gray.
In every heartbeat, in every sigh,
Winter's embrace will always tie.

Winter's Soft Embrace

In winter's arms, the world turns bright,
Snowflakes dance in the soft moonlight.
A blanket of white wraps 'round the trees,
Whispers of joy flowing with the breeze.

Fires glow warm, flickering gold,
Stories of wonder and dreams retold.
Together we gather, hearts open wide,
In this soft embrace, love won't hide.

Glistening paths lead us astray,
Adventures await, come join the play.
With laughter and music, the night unfolds,
In winter's embrace, life's beauty molds.

As stars twinkle bright in the chilly air,
We share the spirit of joy and care.
In every moment, let our hearts race,
Together we find winter's soft grace.

Shimmers of Ice

Glittering crystals in the light,
Dancing like stars in the night.
Laughter echoes through the air,
Joyful moments, beyond compare.

Each flake a wish, each twirl a cheer,
Winter's beauty drawing near.
With friends we gather, hearts so bright,
Embraced in love, a warm delight.

Bonfires crackle, stories share,
Glow of warmth, without a care.
Toasting marshmallows, sweet delight,
Under the blanket of the night.

Shimmers of ice, a wondrous show,
In this season, our spirits glow.
Together we sing, our hearts take flight,
In festive joy, everything feels right.

The Art of Calm

In the hush of twilight's glow,
Gentle breezes begin to flow.
Warm tea brewing, a moment still,
Embracing peace, a tranquil thrill.

Clusters of laughter fill the space,
Soft conversations, a warm embrace.
Candles flicker, shadows dance,
In the glow, we find our chance.

Fleeting time, a soothing art,
Finding joy in every part.
With festive hearts, our worries cease,
In this calm, we discover peace.

The world outside may rush and spin,
But here, it's where the love begins.
Together we breathe, feeling free,
In the art of calm, just you and me.

Soft-Mantled Dreams

Whispers of night in pastel hues,
Wrapped in warmth, like soft morning dew.
Glistening hopes upon the sheets,
Where slumbering magic gently greets.

Stars twinkle softly in the sky,
Painting dreams as they drift by.
A lullaby sung in the breeze,
Filling our hearts with tender ease.

Cups of cocoa, frothy and sweet,
With each sip, our worries retreat.
Around the fire, tales unfold,
In soft-mantled dreams, our hearts are bold.

Embracing comfort, side by side,
In dreamy realms, we joyfully glide.
With each moment, our spirits gleam,
Woven together, this festive dream.

Silence at Dawn

The world awakes in hush and glow,
Softly beneath the morning snow.
Birdsongs linger, sweet and light,
As daybreak whispers, banishing night.

Frosted branches twinkle bright,
Nature's canvas, pure delight.
In this silence, heartbeats blend,
New beginnings, here no end.

Glistening fields stretch far and wide,
Wrapped in beauty, nature's pride.
With joy we greet this vibrant day,
In silence at dawn, we find our way.

Warming tea in hand, we stand,
Together, face the world so grand.
In festive moments, peace we seek,
As the dawn breathes life, tender and meek.

Echoes of a Quiet Hearth

In the glow of amber light,
Laughter fills the gentle night.
Whispers dance like flames that leap,
Memories we hold, forever keep.

Songs of joy and spirits bright,
Gather close, feel love's delight.
Mugs raised high, a toast we share,
Together, lost in warmth and care.

The crackle sings a soothing tune,
As outside, glimmers of the moon.
Hearts entwined, where shadows play,
In this moment, we shall stay.

Softly fades the evening's glow,
Yet in our hearts, the warmth will flow.
Echoes linger, sweet and clear,
In a quiet hearth, we hold dear.

Shadows Cast by Candlelight

Softly flickers, candle bright,
Shadows dance in soft twilight.
Gentle whispers fill the air,
Filling souls with love and care.

Here we gather, hearts aligned,
In the glow, our hopes combined.
Each soft flame tells a story,
Of shared laughter and sweet glory.

Silhouettes of joy take flight,
In a world that feels so right.
Hand in hand, we share the night,
Bathed in the magic of candlelight.

As the stars above so shine,
We celebrate, hearts entwined.
In the warmth of this embrace,
Shadows dance, a sacred space.

Serenity Wrapped in Crystal

In the stillness, crystals glow,
Reflecting dreams, like soft snow.
A gentle hum, the breeze does sing,
Whispers of joy, the season brings.

Wrapped in peace, our hearts take flight,
Every sparkle, pure delight.
Frosted edges, nature's art,
Binding us, never apart.

Laughter dances, high above,
In this realm, we know pure love.
Moments captured, hearts embrace,
In serenity, we find our place.

Crystal dreams that softly gleam,
Fill our souls with hope and beam.
Together here, forever clear,
In this magic, we hold dear.

The Lullaby of the Silent Woods

In the stillness of the trees,
Whispers linger in the breeze.
Nature hums a gentle song,
Where each heart knows it belongs.

Underneath the starry skies,
Dreams awaken, softly rise.
Moonlit paths that gently wind,
Magic waits for us to find.

Crickets play their serenade,
While shadows cast a gentle shade.
In this hush, the world feels right,
Comfort found in the night light.

The woods embrace with open arms,
Drawn to peace and nature's charms.
Lullabies of crickets' calls,
In the silence, joy befalls.

Shadows on Snow

Footprints glimmer in the light,
Children laughing, pure delight.
Snowflakes dance upon the breeze,
Echoing joy through winter trees.

Fireplaces crackle, warmth abounds,
Cheerful carols, joyful sounds.
Lanterns twinkle, stars are bright,
Celebration fills the night.

Cookies baked with love and care,
Gifts exchanged, a moment rare.
Merry voices blend and sway,
In this festive, bright ballet.

With every smile, the heart aglow,
Laughter weaves a radiant show.
Together here, we find our peace,
In winter's charm, the wonders cease.

Soft Sighs of Silence

In the hush of winter's breath,
Softly rests a world beneath.
Blankets white of quiet grace,
Embrace the stillness of this place.

Candles flicker, shadows play,
As dusk descends, the night holds sway.
Whispers of the frost-kissed air,
Wrap us all in tender care.

The joy of friends around the fire,
Hearts ignite with warm desire.
Delicate laughter fills the dark,
Each moment cherished leaves a mark.

A gentle snowfall, pure and bright,
Offers peace on this festive night.
Embracing dreams, let spirits soar,
In silence sweet, we find our core.

Enchanted Spaces

Glowing lights adorn the trees,
Magic whispers on the breeze.
Laughter sparkles in the air,
Joyful moments everywhere.

Ribboned gifts in vibrant hues,
Flavors of the season's muse.
Families gather, hearts held near,
Love and warmth, the time is here.

Snowmen crafted, smiles abound,
In this haven, joy is found.
Share the stories of the past,
In enchanted spaces, bonds are cast.

Songs of cheer, let spirits climb,
In every melody, a rhyme.
Together we'll create a tale,
In festive realms, we shall not fail.

Lullabies of the North

Underneath the starry dome,
Winter calls us to come home.
Wrap your dreams in warm embrace,
Feel the magic in this space.

Snowflakes fall like gentle sighs,
Whispers blend with lullabies.
Fireside tales, with loved ones near,
In this season, joy is clear.

Time slows down as hearts unite,
In the glow of soft moonlight.
The spirit of the night invites,
To dance with wonder as it lights.

Lullabies of peace resound,
In the joy of love, we're found.
As snow blankets the earth's embrace,
Celebrate the magic of this place.

Beneath a Glistening Veil

Beneath a veil of shimmering light,
Laughter dances, hearts take flight.
Colors twirl in the crisp, cool air,
Joyful whispers everywhere.

Sparkling faces, smiles all around,
In the magic, love is found.
Hand in hand, we sway and spin,
Tonight, let the festivities begin.

Candles flicker, stories unfold,
A tapestry of memories bold.
Warm embraces, a festive cheer,
Together we celebrate, drawing near.

As stars peek through the twilight haze,
We'll cherish every twinkling gaze.
Beneath the glistening cloak we share,
Moments woven with joyful care.

Quietude in White

In a world shrouded in winter's white,
Soft snow blankets all in sight.
Whispers of peace fill the chilly air,
Together we find comfort there.

Gentle laughter, children play,
Building dreams in the snow today.
Hot cocoa warms our frosty hands,
In quietude, joy expands.

Candles glow in window frames,
Serene moments - they feel like flames.
Each twinkle sparkles, soft and bright,
Bringing warmth to this tranquil night.

Hearts unite under the starry dome,
In this season, we find our home.
As the world sleeps, we dream and sing,
A festive spirit, a wondrous thing.

Serene Moments

Softly falling, the snowflakes twirl,
In the hush of night, the magic unfurl.
Glowing lights twinkle, a gentle embrace,
In serene moments, we find our place.

Joyful carols echo through the trees,
Melodies linger, carried by the breeze.
With every note, our spirits soar,
Celebrating life, forevermore.

Gathered around the flickering flame,
Each heart beats, forever the same.
We share our stories, laughter, and cheer,
In these moments, love draws near.

Snowflakes shimmer in the moon's soft light,
A tapestry woven through the night.
Together we weave our dreams with care,
In serene moments, joy we share.

Frozen Dreams

Amidst the chill, the world is bright,
Frozen dreams in the soft moonlight.
Nature whispers, a secret tune,
As stars twinkle like silver spoons.

With every breath, the magic grows,
In the glow of warmth, our laughter flows.
Surrounded by friends, old and new,
In this moment, life feels true.

Snowflakes dance in a rhythmic sway,
Creating joy in a playful way.
As we gather, stories unfold,
Moments valuable, more precious than gold.

Together we build a world of cheer,
In frozen dreams, our hearts draw near.
With every smile, we carve our seams,
Creating magic from frozen dreams.

9 789908 116198